PIANO · VOCAL · GUITAR

CHART HITS
OF 2016–2017

ISBN 978-1-4950-9089-9

HAL•LEONARD®

7777 W. BLUEMOUND RD. P.O. BOX 13819 MILWAUKEE, WI 53213

Visit Hal Leonard Online at
www.halleonard.com

BLUE AIN'T YOUR COLOR

Words and Music by HILLARY LINDSEY,
STEVEN LEE OLSEN and CLINT LAGERBERG

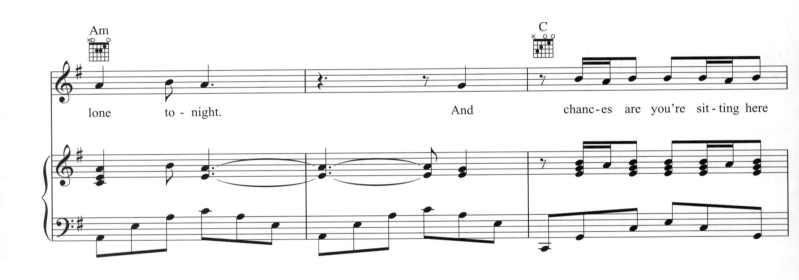

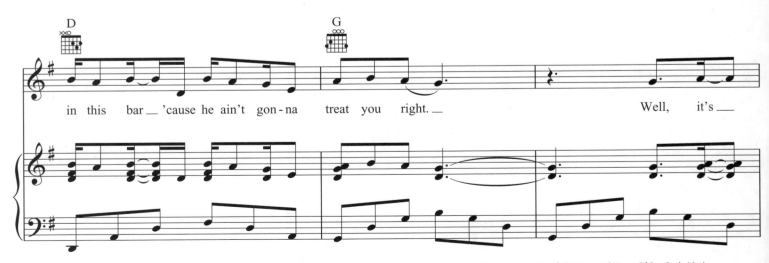

ne - on buzz - ing on the wall, but, dar - ling, it don't match your eyes. _____

I'm tell - ing you, _____ you don't need that guy.

It's so black and white; he's steal - ing your thun - der. ____ Ba - by,

blue ain't your ___ col - or. ___ I'm not tryin' to

CLOSER

Words and Music by ANDREW TAGGART,
ISAAC SLADE, JOSEPH KING, ASHLEY FRANGIPANE,
SHAUN FRANK and FREDERIC KENNETT

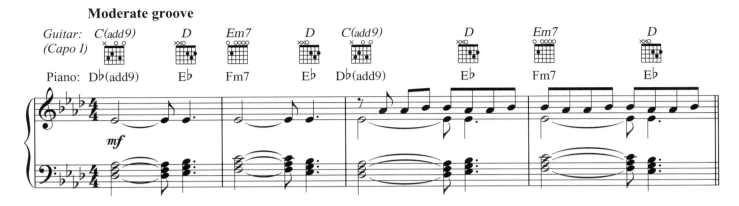

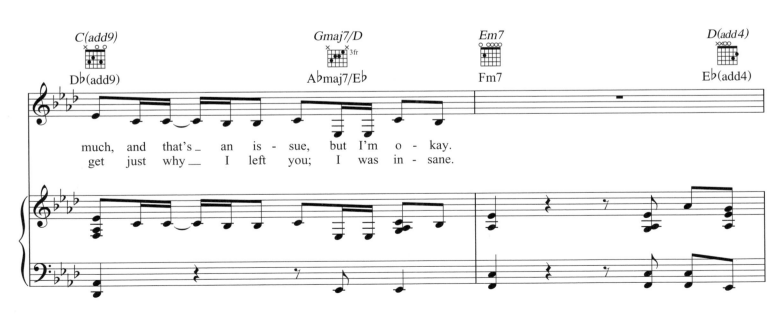

Hey, yeah, tell your friends it was nice to meet __ them, but I
Stay, and play that Blink One - Eight - y - Two __ song that we

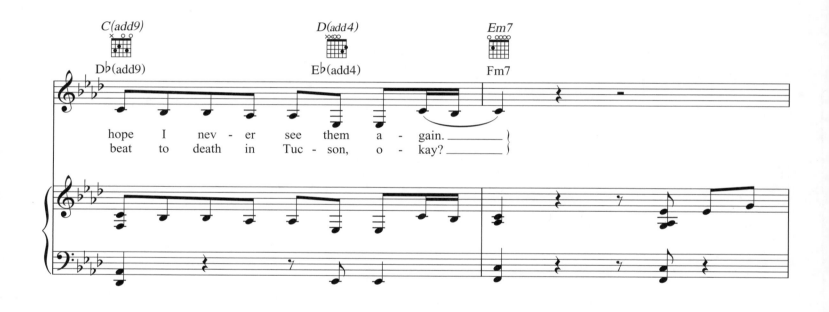

hope I nev - er see them a - gain. ___
beat to death in Tuc - son, o - kay? ___

I know it breaks your heart; moved to the cit - y in a broke - down car and,

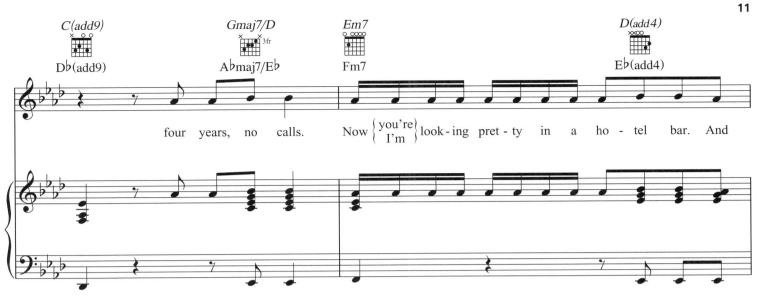

four years, no calls. Now {you're / I'm} look-ing pret-ty in a ho-tel bar. And

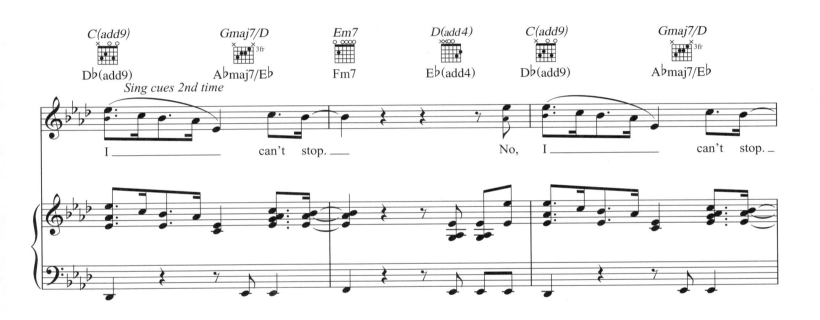

Sing cues 2nd time

I _____ can't stop. _____ No, I _____ can't stop. _

Both 2nd time: So, ba-by, pull me clos-er in the back seat of your Ro-ver that I

know you can't af-ford. Bite that tat-too on your shoul-der, pull the sheets right off the cor-ner of the

mat-tress that you stole from your room-mate back in Boul-der. We ain't ev-er get-tin' old-er.

We ain't

COLD WATER

Words and Music by THOMAS PENTZ,
KAREN ØRSTED, HENRY ALLEN,
JUSTIN BIEBER, BENJAMIN LEVIN,
ED SHEERAN, JAMIE SCOTT
and PHILIP MECKSEPER

Male: I'll be ___ your life - line ___ to - night. ___

___ Female: You won't ___ let go. Male: I'll be ___ your

life - line ___ to - night. ___ I won't let go.

I won't ___ let go.

HANDCLAP

Words and Music by ERIC FREDERIC,
SAMUEL HOLLANDER, MICHAEL FITZPATRICK,
JOSEPH KARNES, JAMES KING,
JEREMY RUZUMNA, NOELLE SCAGGS
and JOHN WICKS

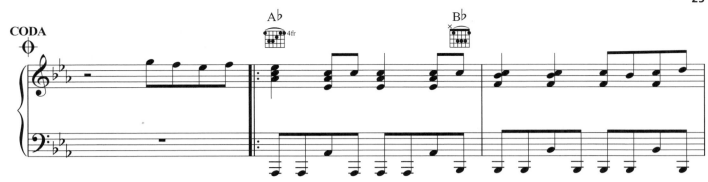

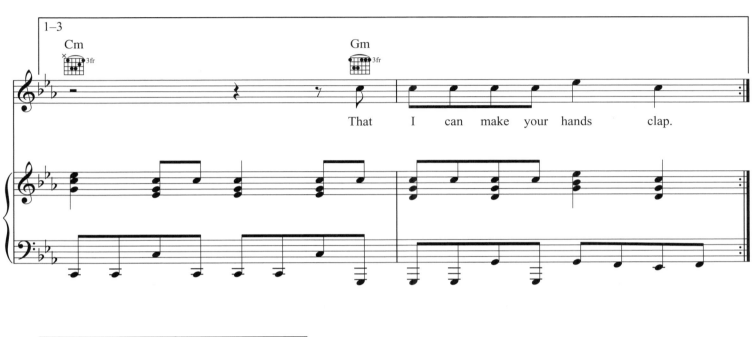

That I can make your hands clap.

So can I get a hand clap?

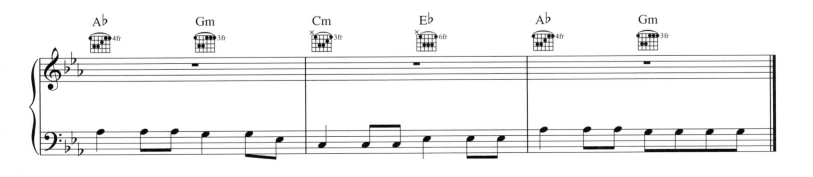

DON'T WANNA KNOW

Words and Music by ADAM LEVINE,
BENJAMIN LEVIN, JOHN HENRY RYAN,
AMMAR MALIK, JACOB KASHER HINDLIN,
ALEX BEN-ABDALLAH, KENDRICK LAMAR,
KURTIS McKENZIE and JON MILLS

Additional Lyrics

Rap: No more "please stop."
No more hashtag boo'd up screenshots.
No more tryna make me jealous on your birthday.
You know just how I make you better on your birthday, oh.
Do he do you like this? Do he woo you like this?
Do he lay it down for you, touch your poona like this?
Matter fact, never mind, we gon' let the past be.
Maybe his right now, but your body's still with me, whoa.

HEATHENS
from SUICIDE SQUAD

Words and Music by
TYLER JOSEPH

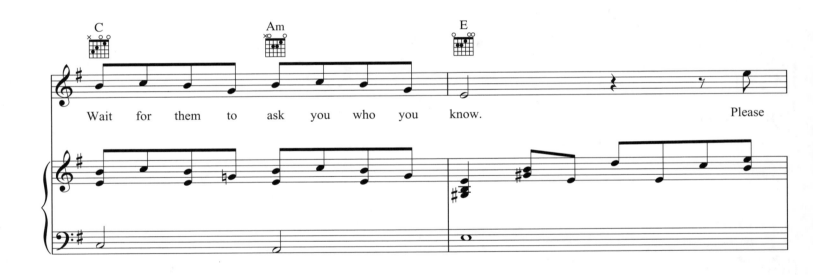

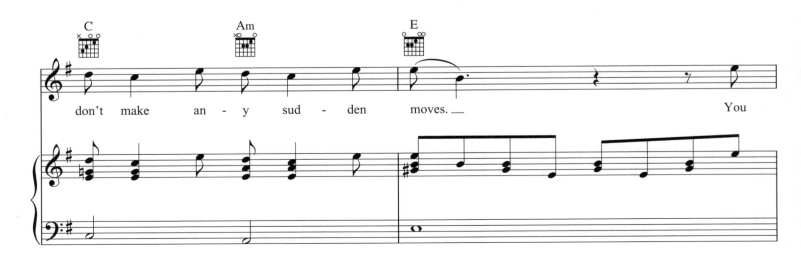

D.S. al Coda

B

you?" But af - ter all I've said, please don't for - get.

CODA

C

We don't deal with out - sid - ers ver - y well. They say new - com - ers have a cer - tain smell.

E5

Am

You have trust is - sues, not to men - tion, they say they can smell your in - ten - tions.

E5

C

Am

E5

You'll nev - er know the freak show sit - ting next to you. You'll have some weird peo - ple sit - ting next to

LET ME LOVE YOU

Words and Music by JUSTIN BIEBER,
CARL ROSEN, WILLIAM GRIGAHCINE,
EDWIN PEREZ, TEDDY MENDEZ,
ANDREW WOTMAN, ALEXANDRA TAMPOSI,
LOUIS BELL, LUMIDEE CEDENO,
BRIAN LEE and STEVEN MARSDEN

Moderate Pop

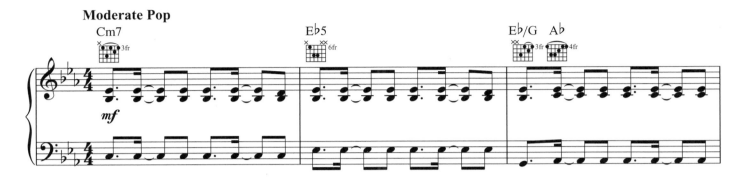

I used to be-lieve _____ we were burn-ing on the edge of some-thing
at the wheel; we've got a mil-lion miles a-

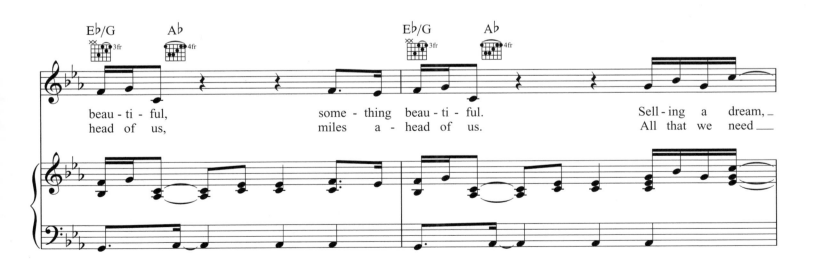

beau-ti-ful, some-thing beau-ti-ful. Sell-ing a dream, _
head of us, miles a-head of us. All that we need _

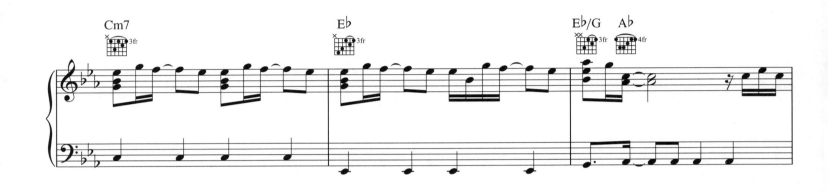

Don't fall a - sleep

Don't you give up, ___ na, ___ na, na. I won't give up, ___ na, ___ na, na. Let ___ me

love you, _ let ___ me love you. _ Don't you give up, ___ na, ___ na, na. I won't give up, _

___ na, ___ na, na. Let ___ me love you, _ let ___ me love you. _

HOW FAR I'LL GO

(Alessia Cara Version)
from MOANA

Music and Lyrics by
LIN-MANUEL MIRANDA

I DON'T WANNA LIVE FOREVER
(Fifty Shades Darker)
from FIFTY SHADES DARKER

Words and Music by TAYLOR SWIFT,
JACK ANTONOFF and SAM DEW

Easy Pop feel

Oh, _____ oh, oh, oh, _____ oh. _____

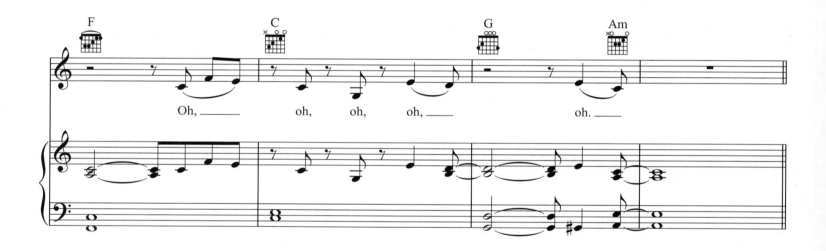

Oh, _____ oh, oh, oh, _____ oh. _____

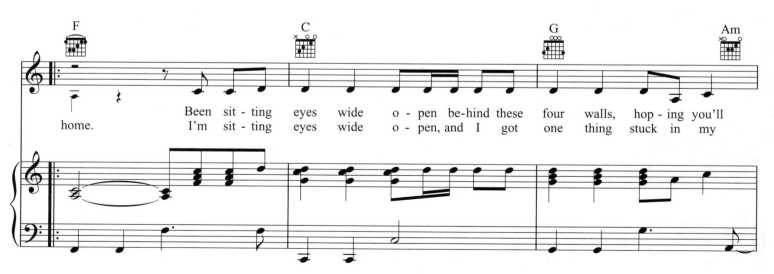

home.   Been sit-ting eyes wide o-pen be-hind these four walls, hop-ing you'll
            I'm sit-ting eyes wide o-pen, and I got one thing stuck in my

LOVE ON THE WEEKEND

Words and Music by
JOHN MAYER

I'm bust - ed up, but I'm lov - ing ev - 'ry min - ute of it.

Love on___ the week - end.___

Love on___ the week - end.___

Repeat and Fade

Optional Ending

MILLION REASONS

Words and Music by STEFANI GERMANOTTA,
MARK RONSON and HILLARY LINDSEY

good one ___ to stay. ___

Oh, ba - by, I'm bleed - in', bleed - in'. ___

Can't you give me what I'm need - in', need - in'?

Ev - 'ry heart - break makes it hard to keep the

SAY YOU WON'T LET GO

Words and Music by STEVEN SOLOMON,
JAMES ARTHUR and NEIL ORMANDY

Moderate Ballad

I met you in the dark, you lit me up,
I wake you up with some break-fast in bed,

you made me feel as though I was e-nough. ___
I'll bring you cof-fee with a kiss on your head. ___

We danced the night a-way,
And I'll take the kids to school,

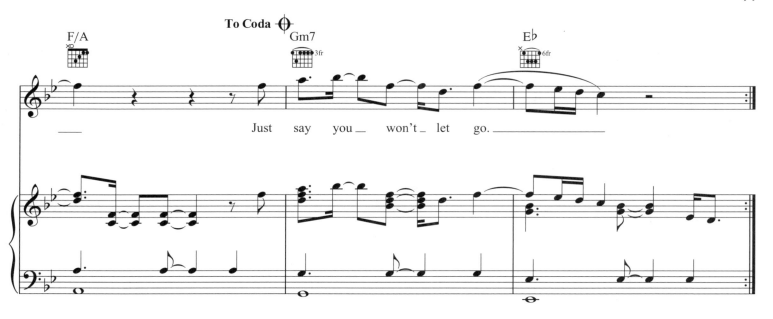

Just say you __ won't __ let __ go. _____

I wan - na live with you __ e - ven when we're ghosts, __

'cause you were al - ways there for me when I need - ed you most. _____

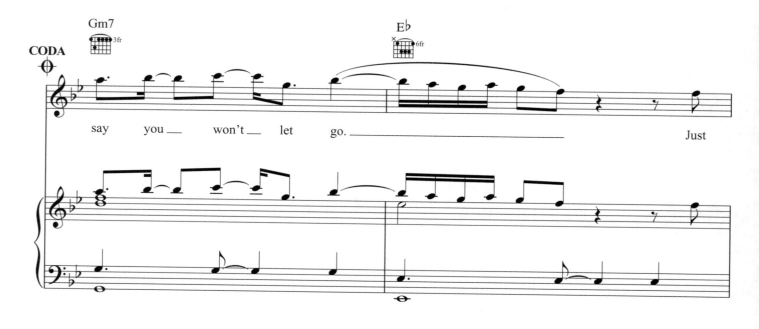

SCARS TO YOUR BEAUTIFUL

Words and Music by ALESSIA CARACCIOLO,
WARREN FELDER, COLERIDGE TILLMAN
and ANDREW WANSEL

Moderate Pop beat

To Coda ⊕

ti - ful. We're stars and we're beau - ti - ful.＿＿＿＿ She has dreams to

be an en - vy, so she's ＿ starv - ing. You know, cov - er girls ＿ eat noth - ing. She says, ＿

＿ "Beau - ty is pain, and there's beau - ty in ev - 'ry - thing. ＿ What's a lit - tle bit of hun - ger?

I can go a lit - tle while long- er." She fades a - way. She don't see her "per - fect," she don't

SEND MY LOVE
(To Your New Lover)

Words and Music by ADELE ADKINS,
MAX MARTIN and SHELLBACK

Moderate groove

This was all you, none of it me, you put your hands on, __ on my bod - y and
I was too strong, you were trem - bling, you could - n't han - dle __ the hot heat

told __ me, __ (ris - ing,) mm, __ told me you were read - y
ris - ing, __ (ris - ing,) mm, __ ba - by, I'm still ris - ing.

THIS TOWN

Words and Music by NIALL HORAN,
MICHAEL NEEDLE, DANIEL BRYER,
and JAMIE SCOTT

Moderately fast Folk feel

With pedal

Wak- ing up ___ to kiss you, ___ and no- bod- y's there. The

smell of ___ your per - fume ___ still stuck in ___ the air. It's

hard. ___

SHAPE OF YOU

Words and Music by ED SHEERAN,
STEVE MAC and JOHN McDAID

SIDE TO SIDE

Words and Music by ARIANA GRANDE,
ONIKA MARAJ, ALEXANDER KRONLUND,
MAX MARTIN, SAVAN KOTECHA and ILYA

Moderately slow Reggae feel

STARBOY

Words and Music by ABEL TESFAYE,
GUY-MANUEL DE HOMEM-CHRISTO,
THOMAS BANGALTER, HENRY WALTER,
MARTIN McKINNEY and JASON QUENNEVILLE